Stop
Raising
Einstein

BY

Tara Kennedy-Kline

A
**UNIQUELY
BRILLIANT**
JOURNAL
ABOUT:

YOUR NAME

Copyright © 2009 by Tara Kennedy-Kline

All rights reserved. No part of this book may be used or reproduced in any manner whatsoever without prior written consent of the author, except as provided by the United States of America copyright law.

Published by Advantage, Charleston, South Carolina.
Member of Advantage Media Group.

ADVANTAGE is a registered trademark and the Advantage colophon is a trademark of Advantage Media Group, Inc.

Printed in the United States of America.

ISBN: 978-1-59932-173-8
LCCN: 2009910803

This publication is designed to provide accurate and authoritative information in regard to the subject matter covered. It is sold with the understanding that the publisher is not engaged in rendering legal, accounting, or other professional services. If legal advice or other expert assistance is required, the services of a competent professional person should be sought.

Most Advantage Media Group titles are available at special quantity discounts for bulk purchases for sales promotions, premiums, fundraising, and educational use. Special versions or book excerpts can also be created to fit specific needs.

For more information, please write: Special Markets, Advantage Media Group, P.O. Box 272, Charleston, SC 29402 or call 1.866.775.1696.

Visit us online at **advantagefamily**.com

What Makes Me Smile

Table of Contents

6 *About This Journal*

8 *Week 1:*
Using Respectful Communication

16 *Week 2:*
Lessons on Integrity

24 *Week 3:*
Setting Goals and Intentions

34 *Week 4:*
Finding Gifts in Our Mistakes

45 *Week 5:*
Live on Purpose

53 *Week 6:*
Focus on Gratitude

64 *Week 7:*
When We Give We Receive

73 *Week 8:*
Twenty-five Things I Love about You

83 *Week 9:*
Live the Life You Dream

94 *Week 10:*
Raising Your Attitude Average

103 *Week 11:*
Creating Your Quiet Space

113 *Week 12:*
Resolve and Resolutions

123 *Afterword*

"The most beautiful thing we can experience is the mysterious. It is the source of all true art and science."

YOUR THOUGHTS ARE YOUR LINK to your dreams, your future, and your heart. When something like a thought or an idea feels important or powerful to you, write it down! Not everything will be a secret key to your future, but it is fun to look back and remind yourself what you were thinking and who you were at a different time in your life.

Journaling is an incredible way to communicate. It can be playful. You and your journal buddy might ask one another what sort of animals you'd want to become if given a choice, or where you'd wake up tomorrow for breakfast. Would it be in Paris or the Serengeti, or would it be on Mars?

Journaling doesn't have to mean writing for hours every night. As a matter of fact, it doesn't even really have to happen at night at all! Some of my best ideas have come to me in the morning or in the middle of the afternoon. Sometimes all I need to write before bed is my list of thanks and a quote that inspired me.

This particular journal is kind of like a training guide to help you begin the process of independent daily journaling. Though you will be learning some very specific tools for communication and living a life of purpose, you can also take the opportunity to write down things that just come up during your conversations. Follow the prompts each day and then let your imagination fly. Eventually, it will become a unique piece of work, just like you!

In the first chapter you will learn about respectful communication and dialogue. This will help you immensely in your work over the next twelve weeks. Although you will be learning new skills and topics, this is definitely one skill you should practice every day for the rest of your journey.

Using Respectful Communication

"Laws alone can not secure freedom of expression; in order that every man present his views without penalty there must be spirit of tolerance in the entire population.."

TARA'S TRUTH #1:
Every person has an opinion and should be allowed to express it without fear of rejection or punishment.

DAILY JOURNALING

This week, take turns using respectful communication. Count to three in your head after someone's last word before you begin to speak.

As you journal each day, be sure to let each person completely finish his or her thought before you respond. If someone interrupts you, patiently remind them that "we do not interrupt" and ask them to allow you to finish your statement before they speak.

In the beginning, it may be necessary to remind them that they will have a turn to talk and you will listen to them until they are finished.

Also, be sure to make an agreement that there are no wrong answers and certainly no critique or correction of anyone's feelings. Then make a promise to follow through and hold up your end of the bargain.

*To get the full value of joy, you must have someone
to divide it with.* —MARK TWAIN

Day One: What was the best thing about my day?

_____

_____

_____

_____

_____

_____

_____

_____

_____

_____

_____

_____

_____

_____

_____

_____

_____

_____

You're blessed when you can show people how to cooperate instead of compete or fight. That's when you discover who you really are, and your place in God's family. —MATTHEW 5:19

Day Two: What was my greatest accomplishment today?

_____

_____

_____

_____

_____

_____

_____

_____

_____

_____

_____

_____

_____

_____

_____

_____

_____

_____

_____

Most of us would be upset if we were accused of being silly. But the word silly comes from the old English word selig and its literal definition is "to be blessed, happy, healthy and prosperous."

Day Three: What made me laugh today?

_____

_____

_____

_____

_____

_____

_____

_____

_____

_____

_____

_____

_____

_____

_____

_____

_____

_____

Finish each day and be done with it. You have done what you could; some blunders and absurdities have crept in; forget them as soon as you can. Tomorrow is a new day; you shall begin it serenely and with too high a spirit to be encumbered with your old nonsense. This day is all that is good and fair. It is too dear, with its hopes and invitations, to waste a moment on yesterdays. —RALPH WALDO EMERSON

Day Four: What frustrated me today and how could I have made it better?

_____

_____

_____

_____

_____

_____

_____

_____

_____

_____

_____

_____

_____

_____

_____

Each of us will one day be judged by our standard of life, not by our standard of living; by our measure of giving, not by our measure of wealth; by our simple goodness, not by our seeming greatness. —WILLIAM A. WARD

Day Five: What would I never change about my life?

_____

_____

_____

_____

_____

_____

_____

_____

_____

_____

_____

_____

_____

_____

_____

_____

_____

_____

_____

Do all the good you can, by all the means you can, in all the ways you can, in all the places you can, at all the times you can, to all the people you can, as long as you ever can. —JOHN WESLEY

Day Six: If I were superhero, I would _____.

_____

_____

_____

_____

_____

_____

_____

_____

_____

_____

_____

_____

_____

_____

_____

_____

_____

_____

_____

_____

Seventh Day Success Story:

* *What did I learn this week?*

_____

_____

_____

_____

_____

* *What were some really cool things that happened when I practiced what I learned?*

_____

_____

_____

_____

* *What would I change?*

_____

_____

_____

_____

* *What would I never want to forget?*

_____

_____

_____

_____

_____

Lessons on Integrity

*"The pursuit of truth and beauty is a sphere of activity
in which we can remain children all our lives.."*

TARA'S TRUTH #2:
We are all responsible for how we react
and the results we create

DAILY JOURNALING

Integrity is doing the right thing even when no one is watching. It is basically being able to recognize what it is that you believe in—and then standing up for it. It's a "say what you mean and mean what you say" kind of thing. If something doesn't feel right for you, or if you're doing something that isn't in alignment with who you are and where you're going, don't do it.

When you do your journaling this week, consider who it is you are "being" in those moments when you have to make a decision or a choice, and then write from that place.

What you don't see with your eyes, don't witness with your mouth. —JEWISH PROVERB

Day One: What does integrity mean to me?

_____

_____

_____

_____

_____

_____

_____

_____

_____

_____

_____

_____

_____

_____

_____

_____

_____

_____

As I grow older, I pay less attention to what men say. I just watch what they do. —ANDREW CARNEGIE

Day Two: What was something I did or said today that made me feel proud?

_____

_____

_____

_____

_____

_____

_____

_____

_____

_____

_____

_____

_____

_____

_____

_____

_____

_____

_____

Be more concerned with your character than your reputation, because your character is what you really are, while your reputation is merely what others think you are. —JOHN WOODEN

Day Three: If someone were describing me, what would I want him or her to say?

_____

_____

_____

_____

_____

_____

_____

_____

_____

_____

_____

_____

_____

_____

_____

_____

_____

_____

Always imitate the behavior of the winner when you lose. —Anonymous

Day Four: What challenge did I face today that I handled with integrity?

_____

_____

_____

_____

_____

_____

_____

_____

_____

_____

_____

_____

_____

_____

_____

_____

_____

_____

Values are like fingerprints. Nobody's are the same, but you leave 'em all over everything you do. —ELVIS PRESLEY

Day Five: What is something I believe in so strongly that I am a marble pillar and cannot be moved?

_____

_____

_____

_____

_____

_____

_____

_____

_____

_____

_____

_____

_____

_____

_____

_____

_____

_____

*Give whatever you are doing and whoever you are
with the gift of your attention.* —JIM ROHN

**Day Six: Describe traits that my family
members have that show integrity.**

_____

_____

_____

_____

_____

_____

_____

_____

_____

_____

_____

_____

_____

_____

_____

_____

_____

_____

Seventh Day Success Story:

* *What did I learn this week?*

_____

_____

_____

_____

_____

* *What were some really cool things that happened when I practiced what I learned?*

_____

_____

_____

_____

* *What would I change?*

_____

_____

_____

_____

* *What would I never want to forget?*

_____

_____

_____

_____

_____

Setting Goals and Intentions

*"There are only two ways to live your life.
One is as though nothing is a miracle. The other
is as though everything is a miracle."*

TARA'S TRUTH #3:
**It's not a parent's job to decide what their children
will become; it is to support and guide them as
they become what they are meant to be.**

ACTIVITY: MY LIFETIME GOALS

"All things are possible if you believe…"—MARK 9:23

Make a list of fifty goals you want to achieve in your life. This list does not have to be completed now, or even this week. Goal lists are living, growing documents and will change and grow as you do! Take some time this week to relax and dream about some of the things you want to accomplish in your lifetime. As you think of new things, add them; and as you accomplish goals on your list, check them off! The greatest thing we can do for our health, happiness, and spirit is to set goals and go after them each day. The bonus is this: Once you have written something down, you have a 200-percent better chance of achieving it! So get started!

In my life, I want to:

Max's Goals:

    Become a chef

    Own a restaurant

    Own a German shepherd and a husky

    Visit Italy

Alex's Goals:

    Be a spaceman

    See a spaceship (rocket)

    Visit Brazil

    Get married

My Goals:

    Visit all 50 states

    Write a book

    Meet Matt Lauer

    Cheer for my sons at their graduations

    Dance with my children at their weddings

DAILY JOURNALING

This week is the perfect opportunity to address issues such as what we do, what we need to do, and what we can skip altogether. The lists that you will create over the next few days will help you identify how you can make your lives easier. It allowed my family to eliminate unessential things that we were cramming into our morning routine. After we figured out what wasn't working, we were able to find a solution that did work.

My 50 Goals:

You can't hit a homerun unless you step up to the plate. You can't catch a fish unless you put your line in the water. You can't reach your goals if you don't try. —Kathy Seligman

Day One: What are the four things I will do tomorrow morning to prepare for my day?

_____

_____

_____

_____

_____

_____

_____

_____

_____

_____

_____

_____

_____

_____

_____

_____

_____

_____

_____

The reason most people never reach their goals is that they don't define them, or ever seriously consider them as believable or achievable. Winners can tell you where they are going, what they plan to do along the way, and who will be sharing the adventure with them. —DENIS WAITLEY

Day Two: Make a list of the activities I must complete tomorrow.

_____

_____

_____

_____

_____

_____

_____

_____

_____

_____

_____

_____

_____

_____

_____

_____

_____

_____

_____

_____

The tragedy of life doesn't lie in not reaching your goal. The tragedy lies in having no goals to reach. —BENJAMIN MAYS

Day Three: From yesterday's list, what didn't I accomplish, what would I move to the top of the list, and what could I have scratched?

_____

_____

_____

_____

_____

_____

_____

_____

_____

_____

_____

_____

_____

_____

_____

_____

_____

_____

All of us perform better and more willingly when we know why we are doing what we have been told or asked to do. —ZIG ZIGLAR

Day Four: What are four things I intend to do tomorrow? For example: Get my homework done before dinner, play a game with my family, pick out six toys to donate to charity, take a bath.

_____

_____

_____

_____

_____

_____

_____

_____

_____

_____

_____

_____

_____

_____

_____

_____

_____

_____

_____

When we are motivated by goals that have deep meaning, by dreams that need completion, by pure love that needs expressing, then we truly live life. —GREG ANDERSON

Day Five: Today, I completed _____ of my four goals. How did that make me feel?

_____

_____

_____

_____

_____

_____

_____

_____

_____

_____

_____

_____

_____

_____

_____

_____

_____

So when you are listening to somebody, completely, attentively, then you are listening not only to the words, but also to the feeling of what is being conveyed, to the whole of it, not part of it. —J. KRISHNAMURTI

Day Six: What was something that went wrong today as a result of not being clear about my intentions? How would I do that over if I could?

_____

_____

_____

_____

_____

_____

_____

_____

_____

_____

_____

_____

_____

_____

_____

_____

_____

_____

_____

_____

Seventh Day Success Story:

* *What did I learn this week?*

_____

_____

_____

_____

_____

* *What were some really cool things that happened when I practiced what I learned?*

_____

_____

_____

_____

* *What would I change?*

_____

_____

_____

_____

* *What would I never want to forget?*

_____

_____

_____

_____

_____

Finding Gifts in Our Mistakes

"Anyone who has never made a mistake has never tried anything new."

TARA'S TRUTH #4:
We must all be allowed to make mistakes or even fail
and suffer the consequences in order to grow.

MAX KLINE HITS THE BALL

Everything happens for a reason, so finding the gifts in our mistakes is important. I believe there are no accidents. Not everybody subscribes to this, and that's okay, but I believe if people are never allowed to make mistakes then they never really learn. Some of the biggest mistakes we make in our lives hold the biggest lessons.

Every person on the planet makes mistakes. Life is messy, but that's the point. The true secret is to find the beauty in the blunder. What keeps us from hitting the ball today—whether it is a mental block or an honest-to-goodness mistake—is what will eventually lead us to hit one out of the park.

ACTIVITY: AFFIRMATION CARDS

"I'm good enough. I'm smart enough, and doggone it, people like me!" —Stuart Smalley

Create a slogan for yourself.

Remember Stuart Smalley standing in front of the mirror spouting those passionate compliments to himself?

That was the start of a wonderful affirmation. My kids call them slogans, but that's okay, too. I actually kind of like that term—"a slogan for myself." That works!

I have many affirmations/slogans that I regularly say to myself and that always serve me well. As a matter of fact, it was an affirmation that saved me many years ago when I was at my lowest point in life.

One of my favorite slogans for me is: "Wherever you go, whatever you do, luck and success go along with you."

I know it sounds a bit cliché, but it was printed on a mug I received as a gift back in 1992, and it has served me well to say it out loud ever since!

Max has found his success with slogans, and anyone on the baseball team can tell you that it works. "Max Kline hits the ball!"

Alex, though he has a quick wit, he also has a sharp tongue. There are times when reacting in anger has gotten him in a lot of trouble. The upside is that he has developed the skill of attention and focus through martial arts. Using the two skills together, he has created the affirmation: "I stop and take a breath before I react."

The whole point behind affirmations or slogans is simply to help us "keep our eyes on the prize" to move us closer to our goals, and to give us a tool to "flip the switch" when we start to lose focus or faith.

So today, we're going to create a slogan (or three) especially for you! To get started, write down the following thoughts.

* Something you want or desire. For instance: "A healthy, 125-pound body."

* Next, write an emotion. It's good to attach a positive emotion to your slogan. Emotions make things powerful. For example: "I am *happily* looking at my healthy, 125-pound body in the mirror."

* A limiting belief or negative thought you carry about yourself in its opposite form. For example: "I cannot do math," would be written as: "I complete my math homework with ease and joy."

Things to remember:

> Keep negative phrases out. In other words, don't repeat what you don't want over and over again.
>
> Make it all about you. You can't make things happen for others, only yourself. (Do this simply by adding the words *I, me,* or your name.)
>
> Keep it simple! "I spread joy and inspiration wherever I go." "I handle every situation with love and patience." "I am thrilled to be at my healthy, goal weight of 125." "I love my family. I love my family."
>
> Whatever works for you...

Now write your slogan on a card or piece of paper and read it out loud.

Have fun with your slogans. They're meant to bring love and more of what you want into your life—and isn't that worth shouting and repeating as a mantra?

DAILY JOURNALING

Each night I ask my kids what went wrong that they might have done differently. It gives them a chance to not only reflect and embrace anything that fate might have thrown their way, but also to figure out what they might do differently next time. They have a chance to own up to their mistakes while also understanding what they need to change. My sons like to imagine putting a problem they don't have control over into a bubble and blowing it away.

This week, when you write in your journal, think of something you did or something that happened each day that made you unhappy with the results. Then journal how you could have done it differently to get the results you would be happy with. Don't focus on the mistakes; they are in the past and cannot be changed. The future and the lessons are your gifts! Make them as bright and beautiful as you dream them to be.

Many of life's failures are people who did not realize how close they were to success when they gave up. —THOMAS EDISON

Day One: What is something that happened today that I would change if I could? How would I change it?

_____

_____

_____

_____

_____

_____

_____

_____

_____

_____

_____

_____

_____

_____

_____

_____

_____

_____

_____

_____

Forgiveness is the answer to the child's dream of a miracle by which what is broken is made whole again, what is soiled is again made clean. —DAG HAMMARSKJOLD

Day Two: What is something that upset me that I have not let go of? Can I let go? When?

_____

_____

_____

_____

_____

_____

_____

_____

_____

_____

_____

_____

_____

_____

_____

_____

_____

_____

Success is failure turned inside out. The silver lining of the clouds of doubt. And you never can tell how close you are, it may be near when it seems so far. So stick to the fight when you're hardest hit. It's when things seem worst that you must not quit. —LILLIAN WHITING

Day Three: What is something that happened today that I must either clean up or put in a bubble, and blow away? What will I do and why?

_____

_____

_____

_____

_____

_____

_____

_____

_____

_____

_____

_____

_____

_____

_____

_____

_____

_____

Constant effort and frequent mistakes are the stepping-stones to genius. —ELBERT HUBBARD

**Day Four: One of my biggest mistakes was
_____. It taught me _____.**

_____

_____

_____

_____

_____

_____

_____

_____

_____

_____

_____

_____

_____

_____

_____

_____

_____

_____

_____

Obstacles don't have to stop you. If you run into a wall, don't turn around and give up. Figure out how to climb it, go through it, or work around it. —MICHAEL JORDAN

Day Five: If I could change two things about myself, what would they be?

_____

_____

_____

_____

_____

_____

_____

_____

_____

_____

_____

_____

_____

_____

_____

Before ending your journaling today, eliminate any negative thoughts by writing them as if they are positive and true for you. For example: "I am not good at math" becomes "I am good at everything when I give my best effort."

Use what talents you possess: the woods would be very silent if no birds sang there except those that sang best. —HENRY VAN DYKE

Day Six: What am I really good at?

_____

_____

_____

_____

_____

_____

_____

_____

_____

_____

_____

_____

_____

_____

_____

_____

_____

_____

Seventh Day Success Story:

* *What did I learn this week?*

_____

_____

_____

_____

_____

* *What were some really cool things that happened when I practiced what I learned?*

_____

_____

_____

_____

_____

* *What would I change?*

_____

_____

_____

_____

* *What would I never want to forget?*

_____

_____

_____

_____

_____

Live on Purpose

"Imagination is more important than knowledge."

TARA'S TRUTH #5:
As parents, we must show children that sometimes it's okay to blur and even cross the lines between dreams and responsibility.

DAILY JOURNALING

I believe that every person on earth has a purpose, and I believe that this purpose is within us from the time we arrive here. I call it a gift. However, I also believe that we're not ready to know it when we're born because as we live our lives and overcome obstacles, we're being taught the tools and lessons we need to eventually truly live our life's purpose.

What I think is kind of cool about doing purpose-hunting exercises is that while you're both finding out those things that you love and that bring joy, energy, and passion into your life, you are also discovering hints and clues to what your purpose is. How amazing will it be in ten years to go back and look at these journals, see those things, and say, "Oh my gosh, I knew it back then. I was on the path to my purpose and I didn't even realize it."

While journaling this week, let your whimsical side come put to play. When it comes to living on purpose—make life an adventure.

The person born with a talent they are meant to use will find their greatest happiness in using it. —JOHANN WOLFGANG VON GOETHE

Day One: The times I have felt the happiest in my life were _____.

_____

_____

_____

_____

_____

_____

_____

_____

_____

_____

_____

_____

_____

_____

_____

_____

_____

_____

_____

Adults are always asking little kids what they want to be when they grow up because they're looking for ideas. —Paula Poundstone

Day Two: If I could do one thing all day long, what would it be?

_____

_____

_____

_____

_____

_____

_____

_____

_____

_____

_____

_____

_____

_____

_____

_____

_____

A span of life is nothing. But the man or woman who lives that span, they are something. They can fill that tiny span with meaning, so its quality is immeasurable, though its quantity may be insignificant. —CHAIM POTOK

Day Three: I think my greatest gifts are _____.

_____

_____

_____

_____

_____

_____

_____

_____

_____

_____

_____

_____

_____

_____

_____

_____

_____

_____

_____

_____

_____

_____

_____

*We all need a daily checkup from the neck up to avoid stinkin' thinkin'
which ultimately leads to hardening of the attitudes.* —ZIG ZIGLAR

Day Four: Others tell me my greatest gifts are _____.

_____

_____

_____

_____

_____

_____

_____

_____

_____

_____

_____

_____

_____

_____

_____

_____

_____

_____

_____

Sometimes in our attempt to give our children what we did not have, we forget to give our children what we did have. —Connie Podesta

Day Five: What are the top ten ways to show me that you love me?

_____

_____

_____

_____

_____

_____

_____

_____

_____

_____

_____

_____

_____

_____

_____

_____

_____

_____

_____

*A friend is a person with whom I may be sincere. Before him
I may think aloud.* —RALPH WALDO EMERSON

Day Six: What are the seven things I would like to do with a friend?

Seventh Day Success Story:

* What did I learn this week?

_____

_____

_____

_____

_____

* What were some really cool things that happened when I practiced what I learned?

_____

_____

_____

_____

* What would I change?

_____

_____

_____

_____

* What would I never want to forget?

_____

_____

_____

_____

Focus on Gratitude

"To know is nothing at all; to imagine is everything."

TARA'S TRUTH #6:
We need to recognize and be grateful for the gifts we receive, no matter where they come from.

FLIP THE SWITCH

No one likes to give a gift to an ungrateful person. Neither does the universe.

The more good we see in the world, the more good we receive in the world. Have you ever had someone tell you something cool about yourself that you hadn't thought of before, and all of a sudden you started to notice that great thing about you getting better and better? Have you ever thought about someone you haven't seen or talked to in awhile, and then suddenly they call you or you run into them somewhere? It's funny how that works, isn't it? It's kind of like you made the request and it was honored!

One way we make sure to bring good things into our lives is to give thanks everyday for the things we appreciate. So as you end each day, acknowledge the gifts you received. You can give thanks in a prayer or in your quiet time or in your journal. But no matter how you do it, do it faithfully each and every day. When you are honest and consistent, you will begin to see your daily gifts grow greater every day.

If you aren't sure what to give thanks for, ask your journal partner to go first and tell you what they are thankful for. You'll probably find that the most precious gifts are not toys or cars or material things. They are more like blessings: a warm bed, a full stomach, sight, laughter, the warmth of the sun, a loving person to read to you and tuck you in. Probably the best gift of all is you! There's nothing wrong with being thankful for whatever brings you joy.

This world has programmed us to complain about anything we don't like or take offense to. It's a true, sad statistic that people will tell seven times more people about a negative experience than they will a positive one. The time is here to flip the switch. Start recognizing the good stuff. Turn on the charm and spread the wealth of a positive attitude.

ACTIVITY: SMILE (SMALL MEMORIES INSPIRING LAUGHTER EVERYDAY) ALBUM

The smile album was inspired when I worked with Discovery Toys. I had a very large team of very fun people. They would send me cards and gifts, and when I did good things they were very generous with their gratitude and their congratulations. I was going through some really tough stuff at the time and would have entire days when I was completely down in the dumps and wouldn't even want to get out of bed. I found myself seeking out those things that would boost me up, those letters of congratulations. I lived for the the expressions that told me the company needed more people like me and that I had made someone believe in him or herself. Those notes made all the difference.

This gave me the idea to collect those things that made me happy and keep them in one place. I got one of those little photo albums and started collecting everything that made me smile—basically, small memories that inspired laughter every day. For example, I had a picture of my little sister Becky when she was really small. We had crimped her hair with one of those crimping irons, and she was wearing a rainbow dress. It was the goofiest looking picture, and it made me laugh hysterically every time I looked at it. I would include a joke of the day that somebody sent me by e-mail, or a picture in a magazine that made me laugh. Anything that raised my spirits went into that album.

I found that just by having one thing I could turn to when I was feeling down in the dumps, I could often change my direction for the entire rest of the day. I think it's really important that everybody have something like that. Everybody has those moments when they're appreciated and recognized, everybody has those things that bring them joy, and I think we need to focus on those things more.

Today, start your own smile album. Paste and copy on the pages at the beginning of the book anything that makes you smile.

DAILY JOURNALING

Starting today, you will be writing at least three things that you are thankful for every day. Think of those things you would like to see more of in your life. If you start to think about the things you DON'T want, quickly turn those thoughts around by thinking of what you appreciate in your life. In other words, instead of writing: *I am thankful that I am not sick*, write down: *I am thankful that I am healthy*.

If you get to three things and you feel like writing more, GO AHEAD! You can never be too thankful. Still, try to make each day different because there are so many things in life to be thankful for!

In difficult times, keep something beautiful in your heart. —JOHN O'DONOHUE

Day One: List three things that I am thankful for today.

_____

_____

_____

_____

_____

_____

_____

_____

_____

_____

_____

_____

_____

_____

_____

_____

_____

_____

All that a man achieves and all that he fails to achieve are the direct result of his own thoughts. —JAMES ALLEN

Day Two: List three things I was thankful for at school or at work today.

_____

_____

_____

_____

_____

_____

_____

_____

_____

_____

_____

_____

_____

_____

_____

_____

_____

_____

_____

_____

*We may run, walk, stumble, drive, or fly, but let us never
lose sight of the reason for the journey or miss a chance to
see a rainbow on the way.* —GLORIA GAITHER

Day Three: List three things I am thankful for in nature.

_____

_____

_____

_____

_____

_____

_____

_____

_____

_____

_____

_____

_____

_____

_____

_____

_____

_____

This bright new day, complete with 24 hours of opportunities, choices, and attitudes comes with a perfectly matched set of 1,440 minutes. This unique gift, this one day, cannot be exchanged, replaced, or refunded. Handle with care. Make the most of it. There is only one to a customer! —JOHN POWELL

Day Four: Did you notice any special gifts you received today?

_____

_____

_____

_____

_____

_____

_____

_____

_____

_____

_____

_____

_____

_____

_____

_____

_____

_____

In ordinary life we hardly realize that we receive a great deal more then we give, and that it is only with gratitude that life becomes rich. —DIETRICH BONHOEFFER

Day Five: Did I rediscover anything in my life that I had taken for granted?

_____

_____

_____

_____

_____

_____

_____

_____

_____

_____

_____

_____

_____

_____

_____

_____

_____

_____

_____

A strong positive mental attitude will create more miracles than any wonder drug. —PATRICIA NEAL

Day Six: List three things I am thankful for in regards to my family.

Seventh Day Success Story:

* *What did I learn this week?*

_____

_____

_____

_____

_____

* *What were some really cool things that happened when I practiced what I learned?*

_____

_____

_____

_____

* *What would I change?*

_____

_____

_____

_____

* *What would I never want to forget?*

_____

_____

_____

_____

_____

When We Give
We Receive

"Only a life lived in the service to others is worth living."

TARA'S TRUTH #7:
Getting is good, but giving is better.

ACTIVITY: LETTERS OF GRATITUDE

This week, take some time to sit down and write a letter of thanks for something someone did for you or someone else. Whether it is a family member, teacher, leader, co-worker, friend, or someone at a business you've recently visited. Tell them the things you appreciate about them. Be as free with your praise as you would with your concerns, and pay extra special attention to the reaction you get both from them and yourself.

Another thing you can do this week is to brainstorm some ideas of how you can help a person or organization in need. What is a gift, talent, or item you can share to make someone else's life better and make a difference? Is there someone whose life would be a little better by simply sharing the gift of your time and presence?

DAILY JOURNALING

Philanthropy derives from Ancient Greek. It means, "to love people." It is any activity intended to promote goodness or improve our quality of life. When we do or give freely to help another person it's called philanthropy.

James Keller said, "A candle loses nothing by lighting another candle." Can you imagine how great it would be if everyone in the world gave a little bit of whatever they could every day? I believe that would surely make this world a better place for everyone. Don't you? When we give of ourselves without any expectation, we open ourselves up to receive more in life. When we give, we feel better and are happier, and the people we help feel better and are happier, too! And as we have already learned, when we are happy and positive, we attract happy, positive people and things to our lives!

Now it's your turn to start changing the world. Each day, list at least three things you did for someone else that day. It could be something big like donating your unused clothing and toys to a shelter or charity, or something not as big but just as important, like helping to clean up after dinner without being asked. No matter what it is, choose something that you did strictly for someone else that made you both feel happy.

Congratulations! You are a philanthropist!

We cannot hold a torch to light another's path without brightening our own. —Ben Sweetland

Day One: What is something I did for someone else today?

_____

_____

_____

_____

_____

_____

_____

_____

_____

_____

_____

_____

_____

_____

_____

_____

_____

_____

_____

_____

Give more than you think is necessary and you will get more than you think you deserve. —TARA KENNEDY-KLINE

Day Two: If I had all the money in the world I would _____ .

_____

_____

_____

_____

_____

_____

_____

_____

_____

_____

_____

_____

_____

_____

_____

_____

_____

_____

_____

Don't be reluctant to give of yourself generously. It is the mark of caring and compassion and personal greatness. —BRIAN TRACY

Day Three: What is something I can do or give to help someone else?

_____

_____

_____

_____

_____

_____

_____

_____

_____

_____

_____

_____

_____

_____

_____

_____

_____

_____

Remember, there is no such thing as a small act of kindness. Every act creates a ripple with no logical end. —SCOTT ADAMS

Day Four: What act of generosity did I witness today?

_____

_____

_____

_____

_____

_____

_____

_____

_____

_____

_____

_____

_____

_____

_____

_____

_____

_____

Value is in the doer, not the deed. —DENIS WAITLEY

**Day Five: I will make a goal to do _____ good
things tomorrow. Describe one.**

_____

_____

_____

_____

_____

_____

_____

_____

_____

_____

_____

_____

_____

_____

_____

_____

_____

_____

There is no greater joy, nor greater reward than to make a fundamental difference in someone's life. —MARY ROSE McGEADY

Day Six: What was the greatest thing I did for someone this week?

_____

_____

_____

_____

_____

_____

_____

_____

_____

_____

_____

_____

_____

_____

_____

_____

_____

_____

Seventh Day Success Story:

* What did I learn this week?

_____

_____

_____

_____

_____

** What were some really cool things that
happened when I practiced what I learned?*

_____

_____

_____

_____

_____

* What would I change?

_____

_____

_____

_____

* What would I never want to forget?

_____

_____

_____

_____

_____

Twenty-five Things
I Love about You

"Love is a better teacher than duty."

TANA'S TRUTH #8:
Sometimes the only thing a child needs from us to help them
make a good choice is to know that they are loved unconditionally.

ACTIVITY: LOVE BOX

An activity to do either with or for someone you love is to make a treasure chest of "things I love about you." Imagine someone you love waking up each day and lifting the lid of their treasure chest, pulling out a random slip of paper, and opening it. On the paper is written, "I love to hear you sing in your room." It sounds ridiculous, but it's just one of the many things you love about that person…and to them, it means the world.

You will need:

- Some quiet time and a place to work

- A pad of paper

- A pen, pencil, or crayon

- Scissors

- An empty box (tissue boxes work really well, but you can get fancy if you'd like.)

- Decorations for your box

- An open mind and a loving heart

Sit down with your pad of paper and think about someone you want to "gift" your loving thoughts to. Write one thing you love about this person (or respect or admire…) on each line. When you have written at least twenty-five things, cut each line so that you have one sentiment on each strip of paper. (For instance, *I love the way you sing while you cook. I love the way you tie your shoes.*) Fold each strip to make a little box or package. Decorate your box with paper or stickers or whatever you'd like. Put the little bundles in the box. Write the instructions on a card or on the box.

This is a treasure chest for when you feel blue.

Reach in a grab one then here's what to do:

Open and read it and know that it's true.

Each treasure is something I love about you.

DAILY JOURNALING

I was blessed with two sets of parents for nearly all my life. But I didn't always see it that way. My parents divorced before I was two years old and by the time I was four they had formed new relationships with my stepparents. I realize now that I had the best of both worlds as a result, but at the time, I resented my stepparents immensely. I always believed they were trying to change me or control me and I made it very clear to them that they were NOT my parents. I remember on my tenth birthday, my step dad, Raymond with whom I had a particularly strained relationship, gave me a book (now that I recall, it was a journal!). In the front of the book he had written a message to me. It said, "Dear Tara, Happy Birthday to a wonderful girl. I have always loved you as if you were my own daughter. With Love, Raymond"

It was short and simple and took six years to say, but those words changed me that day, as well as the way I will look at him forever. From that moment, I loved him, too.

You may want to take this opportunity to share ten things you love about your journal partner and have them write down what you say, then have them do the same for you. It's amazing how much you are loved!

Kindness is more important than wisdom, and the recognition of this is the beginning of wisdom. —THEODORE ISAAC RUBIN

Day One: What does love mean to me?

_____

_____

_____

_____

_____

_____

_____

_____

_____

_____

_____

_____

_____

_____

_____

_____

_____

_____

_____

When we seek to discover the best in others, we somehow bring out the best in ourselves. —WILLIAM ARTHUR WARD

Day Two: What are my favorite things about my best friend?

_____

_____

_____

_____

_____

_____

_____

_____

_____

_____

_____

_____

_____

_____

_____

_____

_____

_____

Life is made of memorable moments. We must teach ourselves to really live...to love the journey not the destination. —ANNA QUINDLEN

Day Three: What are five small things I noticed about my teacher, boss, or partner that made a huge and wonderful impact on my day today?

_____

_____

_____

_____

_____

_____

_____

_____

_____

_____

_____

_____

_____

_____

_____

_____

_____

_____

_____

_____

Every person ever created is so special that their presence in the world makes it richer and fuller and more wonderful than it could ever have been without them. —JOHN RUSKIN

Day Four: Think of someone doing a job, whether it is a soldier or a hairdresser. Write them a letter telling them what a great job they did.

_____

_____

_____

_____

_____

_____

_____

_____

_____

_____

_____

_____

_____

_____

_____

_____

_____

Never look down on anybody, unless you are helping them up. —JESSE JACKSON

Day Five: Name someone who has bothered me lately. Ten things that I like or admire about him or her are: _____.

_____

_____

_____

_____

_____

_____

_____

_____

_____

_____

_____

_____

_____

_____

_____

_____

*Did you stop at ten? How did you feel about that person
when you were finished? Keep the list, and the next time
you are feeling frustrated with that person, read it.*

When you choose to be pleasant and positive in the way you treat others, you have also decided, in most cases, how you are going to be treated by others. —ZIG ZIGLAR

Day Six: What was something cool that happened when I approached a troubled relationship with a fresh perspective?

_____

_____

_____

_____

_____

_____

_____

_____

_____

_____

_____

_____

_____

_____

_____

_____

_____

_____

Seventh Day Success Story:

* *What did I learn this week?*

_____

_____

_____

_____

_____

* *What were some really cool things that happened when I practiced what I learned?*

_____

_____

_____

_____

_____

* *What would I change?*

_____

_____

_____

_____

* *What would I never want to forget?*

_____

_____

_____

_____

Live the Life You Dream

"Imagination is everything. It is the preview of life's coming attractions."

TARA'S TRUTH #9:
Every child should be allowed to dream. It comes naturally
to them, and as parents, we mustn't interfere. If children
learn through play, they grow through dreams.

IMAGINE THE POSSIBILITES

When we dream, we are basically telling ourselves that we believe in our own abilities and we want to achieve the greatest "self" we are capable of. Some people believe that it is selfish to dream. I believe that we cannot truly find ourselves unless we dream!

Our dreams can allow and even teach us to be extremely generous. The more we fill our lives with passion and abundance through our dreams, the more we will have to share and give to others. I've been criticized for dreaming of becoming a millionaire, to which I've often said, "If I want to donate a million dollars to charity, I must first acquire a million dollars!" Does that make me selfish for dreaming of being a millionaire?

As we achieve our own dreams, we develop the ability to help others achieve their dreams, too. Imagine what a beautiful world that would be!

I want to encourage you to take some time to let yourself imagine the possibilities of your life. Don't just think about what is realistic. Consider what might seem nearly outrageous about what would require you to grow and move beyond who it is you currently know yourself to be. Think about what you have always wanted to do, be, or have in your life, and listen carefully to those things that come to you in your thoughts and dreams.

My favorite quote from a song is from Michael Jackson's "Man in the Mirror." It goes, "If you want to make the world a better place, take a look at yourself, and then make that change." If you want change in your life, it's up to you! When you want something you've never had, you've got to do something you've never done. You decide. You get to choose your thoughts. Try giving big thought and energy to the direction of your life and who you want to be as a son/daughter, a sibling, and a person. Create your own success story!

During this process, I am going to ask you to think outside the box. That might mean owning an island in the South Pacific, or it might be a more loving, stress-free relationship with your family. Whatever it is, don't hold back! Be outrageous and let your imagination fly. This does not mean thinking unrealistic, pie-in-the-sky stuff, like being able to fly or grow six inches in a day; it simply means allowing yourself to stretch and believe in the possibility of your dreams.

ACTIVITY: VISION BOARD

This is one of the coolest activities we do together as a family because it lets us explore together, the beauty of our dreams!

Besides a large area to work, an open mind, and a playful spirit, you will need:

- Poster board, display board, cork board

- Pencils, markers, crayons, paint, etc.

- Pictures, words, phrases, quotes—anything that inspires you to think about your dreams

- Glue or tape

First divide your poster into four sections: My Dreams for What I Want to Do, Be, Give and Have. Cut out pictures and words that remind you of your dream goals and then place those cutouts on your poster in one of the four sections.

For example, under What I Want to Do, I have pictures of places I want to vacation, trips I have taken with my kids, and the words "Dream & Travel," to name a few. Under What I Want to Be, I have pictures of my mentors, both spiritual and professional, a mock-up of my speaker ad as well as a PhotoShopped picture of my head on my dream body. Under What I Want to Have are pictures of my dream yard, my dream car, and my friends, and under What I Want to Give, I have Monopoly money, pictures of baskets of food, toys, and medication next to the names and logos of the charities I support.

Have fun with this project, and whatever you do—dream big! Because really, what's the worst thing that could happen if you achieved everything you dreamed of? Remember: It's not the size of the dream but the effort you put into achieving it that makes you great!

DAILY JOURNALING

This week, I want you to pretend that you are watching a movie in which you are the star. Close your eyes and see each dream being played out in 4-D. See each place, person, and action in full color. Hear the sounds, feel the breezes, taste the flavors, and experience the emotions of everything around you.

For the next few days, open your mind and share what happens in the screen adaption of your perfect life.

Dreams come true; without that possibility, nature would not incite us to have them. —JOHN UPDIKE

Day One: What is my perfect day?

_____

_____

_____

_____

_____

_____

_____

_____

_____

_____

_____

_____

_____

_____

_____

_____

_____

_____

_____

It's not what you know but what you believe that determines your success in life. —TARA KENNEDY-KLINE

Day Two: What will I be when I grow up?

_____

_____

_____

_____

_____

_____

_____

_____

_____

_____

_____

_____

_____

_____

_____

_____

_____

_____

_____

_____

All men dream but not equally. Those who dream by night in the dusty recesses of their minds wake in the day to find that it was vanity; but the dreamers of the day are dangerous men, for they may act their dream with open eyes to make it possible. —T.E. LAWRENCE

Day Three: If there were no limits (like time, money or support of my family and friends) , what would I do?

_____

_____

_____

_____

_____

_____

_____

_____

_____

_____

_____

_____

_____

_____

_____

_____

_____

_____

Cherish your visions and your dreams, as they are the children of your soul, the blueprints of your ultimate achievements. —NAPOLEON HILL

Day Four: What do I dream for me?

_____

_____

_____

_____

_____

_____

_____

_____

_____

_____

_____

_____

_____

_____

_____

_____

_____

_____

_____

_____

_____

We dream so we don't have to be apart so long. If we're in each other's dreams, we can play together all night. —BILL WATTERSON

Day Five: My dream for you, my journal buddy, is _____.

_____

_____

_____

_____

_____

_____

_____

_____

_____

_____

_____

_____

_____

_____

_____

_____

_____

_____

_____

*The future belongs to those who believe in the beauty
of their dreams.* —ELEANOR ROOSEVELT

Day Six: What does my perfect world look like?

_____

_____

_____

_____

_____

_____

_____

_____

_____

_____

_____

_____

_____

_____

_____

_____

_____

_____

_____

_____

_____

Seventh Day Success Story:

* *What did I learn this week?*

_____

_____

_____

_____

_____

* *What were some really cool things that happened when I practiced what I learned?*

_____

_____

_____

_____

_____

* *What would I change?*

_____

_____

_____

_____

* *What would I never want to forget?*

_____

_____

_____

_____

_____

Raising Your Attitude Average

"Most people say that it is the intellect which makes a great scientist. They are wrong: it is character."

TARA'S TRUTH #10:
We need to be aware of who we are becoming and what we are creating based on the people we surround ourselves with—and we must be willing to adjust this when necessary.

BLESS AND RELEASE

One of the things that I found to be extremely beneficial with my kids was the concept that we're the average of the five people we spend the most time with. It is all up to us. We either become or create the average attitude of the people we spend the most time with.

When there are times that we need to completely change the company we keep, it becomes a matter of blessing and releasing those people. At the end of the day, it is imperative that we create our own circle of excellence.

DAILY JOURNALING

This week while you are journaling, consider what you would want to hear people saying about you if you were standing right outside their door. When you talk about the people you admire, do they have those same traits and gifts?

As my hero Jack Canfield says: Are they the kind of person who lights up a room when they walk in or when they walk out?

Trust men and they will be true to you; treat them greatly and they will show themselves great. —RALPH WALDO EMERSON

Day One: My five heroes are _____.
They're my heroes because _____.

_____

_____

_____

_____

_____

_____

_____

_____

_____

_____

_____

_____

_____

_____

_____

_____

_____

_____

_____

_____

_____

If we want our children to possess the traits of character we most admire, we need to teach them what those traits are and why they deserve both admiration and allegiance. —WILLIAM J. BENNETT

Day Two: My best friends are _____. What I like best about them is _____.

_____

_____

_____

_____

_____

_____

_____

_____

_____

_____

_____

_____

_____

_____

_____

_____

_____

_____

_____

Keep away from people who try to belittle your ambitions. Small people always do that, but the really great make you feel that you too can become great. —MARK TWAIN

Day Three: If I could choose five people to take on an adventure, who would they be?

_____

_____

_____

_____

_____

_____

_____

_____

_____

_____

_____

_____

_____

_____

_____

_____

_____

_____

_____

_____

_____

The best index to a person's character is (a) how he treats people who can't do him any good, and (b) how he treats people who can't fight back. —ABIGAIL VAN BUREN

Day Four: The five most important people on the planet are _____.

_____

_____

_____

_____

_____

_____

_____

_____

_____

_____

_____

_____

_____

_____

_____

_____

_____

_____

_____

_____

We judge ourselves by what we feel capable of doing, while others judge us by what we have already done. —HENRY WADSWORTH LONGFELLOW

Day Five: Who is someone I see every day but don't know anything about? What are five questions I would like to ask them?

_____

_____

_____

_____

_____

_____

_____

_____

_____

_____

_____

_____

_____

_____

_____

_____

_____

_____

_____

_____

*The question for the child is not do I want to be good? But
whom do I want to be like?* —Bruno Bettelheim

Day Six: I would love to spend more time with _____.

_____

_____

_____

_____

_____

_____

_____

_____

_____

_____

_____

_____

_____

_____

_____

_____

_____

_____

Seventh Day Success Story:

* *What did I learn this week?*

_____

_____

_____

_____

_____

* *What were some really cool things that
happened when I practiced what I learned?*

_____

_____

_____

_____

_____

* *What would I change?*

_____

_____

_____

_____

* *What would I never want to forget?*

_____

_____

_____

_____

_____

Creating Your Quiet Space

*"Not everything that can be counted counts, and
not everything that counts can be counted."*

TARA'S TRUTH #11:
**Time out should be for both the child and the
caretaker. It is more important that it be a space to
regroup and decompress than punish the child.**

ACTIVITY: CREATE YOUR FOCUS SPACE

I have realized that when tempers flare in my house, it's usually because someone is either hungry, frustrated, or needs a nap, so they are throwing a tantrum—and it's not always the kids! For that reason, I believe that time out should be the discipline of choice, and it should be *for adults and children*!

When I am ready to lose my temper with my kids, I will typically say something like this: "It's obvious we need a break from each other. Everyone to their rooms for ten minutes." I started timing by age, one minute for every year, but eventually they began to fight over that, too, so now it's ten minutes because that's easy.

After the ten minutes is up, we don't talk about the problem again unless we need to clear something up in order to be present for each other. We also make it very clear that if we do need to discuss an issue, the conversation must be positive and productive. If not, we "put it in a bubble and blow it away." The end.

This process has worked really well for us because (a) we stick to it, and (b) we have created a space for ourselves that allows us to relax and do what we love. The boys have their music, art materials, pets, and books in their rooms because that's their space to spend their "quiet time." I have also found that it is much easier for them to fall asleep at night because they have chosen to keep in their rooms the things that quiet their minds.

My space has a comfy chair, my favorite books, my exercise equipment, and my CD player as well as candles and chocolate. Creating these spaces and using them faithfully has been a real blessing to our family. It's taught us how to decompress before we blow and has served to help us avoid many, many situations that could have led to bad choices and regrettable behavior.

DAILY JOURNALING

One of my teachers Arthur Joseph, who is the founder of the Vocal Awareness Institute, taught me the skill of "allowing a deep loving breath." I think that one of the most relaxing and calming things I have ever done is to simply learn how to breathe.

Take a deep breath. Did you feel you're your neck tighten and hear the noise the air made when you breathed in? Now close your eyes and think the words "I love you" while you "allow" the next breath. Notice the difference?

I call this relaxed breathing and you should practice it in your quiet time. In addition, find something positive or funny that you can focus on in the time it takes to breathe. Can you see how you can use these techniques to change your mood in a single breath?

Each day, take time to quiet your mind and focus on the events of your day. Picture it as if it had gone perfectly for you. Think of something that left you feeling confused or stuck and then in your quiet time, ask for guidance on how you can solve that problem as your greatest self. Focus on your breathing. When you are ready, open your eyes and share your thoughts with your journal partner.

Take your quiet time before you journal today. Write whatever comes into your mind when you open your eyes.

Happiness isn't something that depends on our surroundings. It's something we make inside ourselves. —CORRIE TEN BOOM

Day One: Where do I feel safe?

_____

_____

_____

_____

_____

_____

_____

_____

_____

_____

_____

_____

_____

_____

_____

_____

_____

_____

_____

_____

_____

*If we are to reach real peace in this world...we shall
have to begin with the children.* —Gandhi

Day Two: When I am angry, I would like it if I could _____.

_____

_____

_____

_____

_____

_____

_____

_____

_____

_____

_____

_____

_____

_____

_____

_____

_____

_____

To the mind that is still, the whole Universe surrenders. —LAO TZU

Day Three: The best way for me to calm down is _____.

_____

_____

_____

_____

_____

_____

_____

_____

_____

_____

_____

_____

_____

_____

_____

_____

_____

_____

No problem can be solved from the same level of consciousness that created it. —ALBERT EINSTEIN

Day Four: If I am in trouble, what is my biggest fear?

_____

_____

_____

_____

_____

_____

_____

_____

_____

_____

_____

_____

_____

_____

_____

_____

_____

_____

_____

No one has yet fully realized the wealth of sympathy, kindness, and generosity hidden in the soul of a child. The effort of every true education should be to unlock that treasure. —EMMA GOLDMAN

Day Five: What is it that frustrates me the most in life?

Imagination was given to us to compensate for what we are not; a sense of humor was given to us to console us for what we are. —MACK McGINNIS

Day Six: Something you could say or do to help me focus is _____.

_____

_____

_____

_____

_____

_____

_____

_____

_____

_____

_____

_____

_____

_____

_____

_____

_____

_____

_____

_____

Seventh Day Success Story:

* *What did I learn this week?*

_____

_____

_____

_____

_____

* *What were some really cool things that
happened when I practiced what I learned?*

_____

_____

_____

_____

_____

* *What would I change?*

_____

_____

_____

_____

* *What would I never want to forget?*

_____

_____

_____

_____

_____

Resolve and Resolutions

"The only source of knowledge is experience."

TARA'S TRUTH #12:
It's easy to make promises to people if we believe they will never remember what we said, but the truth is, people never truly forget. And those promises, whether kept or broken, will determine the integrity with which they live their lives.

DO YOU WANT TO SAVE THE CHANGES YOU HAVE MADE?

If you've ever written a paper or done any kind of work on a computer, you know that when you get ready to close the program the computer throws you a pretty serious reminder. It asks you, "Do you want to save the changes you have made?"

Now that you have come to the end of this program and have hopefully made some pretty significant amendments to your life, you have a choice to make. I am going to ask you to make an agreement—not with me, but with yourself and your journal partner. It would be so much easier to maintain the status quo, but instead, will you agree to "save the changes you have made" and continue to live a life of respect, integrity, intention, purpose, and dreams?

If so, let me be the first to thank you, because you are among the dreamers and are bound to make a difference in the world.

It's easy when things are romantic and we're in a honeymoon period to make that commitment and say, "This is what I'm going to do for the rest of my life." What's difficult is following through to make the changes you've made a part of your life and who you are.

I've stopped making New Year's resolutions because I've realize that I should be making resolutions constantly, not just one day a year. What I found during the journaling process with my kids was that I set little resolutions frequently. These were things that were so vital and so important to my family and the way that we move forward that failure was not an option. It is something that I've been doing for an entire year.

If this three-month journaling journey has made a change in your life, if you've seen a difference in the way you play together, the way you talk to others, and the way you have respect for each other, then make that commitment to make it a part of each day. The best way to do this is to take a look at where you were when you started. See how far you've come, and decide to make it a journey forward rather than a step back. Once you've got that momentum, it's a lot easier to keep moving in the right direction.

How has journaling changed you? How are you a better person? What have you learned about your journal buddy? What does your life look like a year from now?

My hope is that you've realized through the course of this process that regardless of how old you are, where you've been, or what you're doing in life, *you have the power to make changes within yourself.* By becoming that person, you're guiding your life in a way you may have never thought you would go, and the sky is the limit. Be the person you were meant to be. Celebrate your unique brilliance and start celebrating the unique brilliance in everyone you meet.

DAILY JOURNALING

You have spent the last eleven weeks exploring new concepts and ideas and realizing the uniqueness that is you. Spend this next week reflecting on what you have learned as well as preparing for what you would like your life to become as you venture on as a Brilliant Dreamer.

Learn from yesterday, live for today, hope for tomorrow. The important thing is not to stop questioning. —ALBERT EINSTEIN

Day One: How has keeping a journal changed how I approach life?

_____

_____

_____

_____

_____

_____

_____

_____

_____

_____

_____

_____

_____

_____

_____

_____

_____

_____

_____

If there is anything we wish to change in the child, we should first examine it and see whether it is not something that could better be changed in ourselves. —CARL JUNG

Day Two: What have I learned about my journal buddy that I didn't know three months ago?

_____

_____

_____

_____

_____

_____

_____

_____

_____

_____

_____

_____

_____

_____

_____

_____

_____

Ideals are like stars; you will not succeed in touching them with your hands. But like the seafaring man on the desert of waters, you choose them as your guides, and following them you will reach your destiny. —CARL SCHURZ

Day Three: What does my life look like a year from now?

_____

_____

_____

_____

_____

_____

_____

_____

_____

_____

_____

_____

_____

_____

_____

_____

_____

_____

_____

_____

_____

_____

Be happy. Talk happiness. Happiness calls out responsive gladness in others. There is enough sadness in the world without yours…never doubt the excellence and permanence of what is yet to be. Join the great company of those who make the barren places of life fruitful with kindness. Your success and happiness lie in you…the great enduring realities are love and service…resolve to keep happy and your joy and you shall form an invincible host against difficulties. —HELEN KELLER

Day Four: Tell a story that celebrates you.

Don't let the fear of striking out keep you from playing the game.

Day Five: Free reign, tell a story that you want to share.

_____

_____

_____

_____

_____

_____

_____

_____

_____

_____

_____

_____

_____

_____

_____

_____

_____

_____

_____

With our thoughts we make the world. —BUDDHA

Day Six: How do you plan to make a difference in the world?

_____

_____

_____

_____

_____

_____

_____

_____

_____

_____

_____

_____

_____

_____

_____

_____

_____

_____

_____

Seventh Day Success Story:

* *What did I learn this week?*

_____

_____

_____

_____

_____

* *What were some really cool things that happened when I practiced what I learned?*

_____

_____

_____

_____

_____

* *What would I change?*

_____

_____

_____

_____

* *What would I never want to forget?*

_____

_____

_____

_____

_____

Mahatma Gandhi said, "Be the change you want to see in the world."

For over a year I have kept a journal with both of my sons. Though each boy has his own style and practices, this process has absolutely transformed our lives.

Through journaling, I've realized that I could spend the rest of my life being sad about all the things that happened to me, or I could spend the rest of my life pursuing my dreams, giving thanks for those people and things that I do have in my life, and making the best life for me and my family.

I now see the gifts in me. I see the gifts in my spouse, and I see the gifts in my children.

Now, although there have been monumental changes, my life certainly isn't perfect. I can't say that we don't ever struggle or disagree. We don't always make the right choices. And sometimes it's not easy to see the gifts in the mistakes we make right away. But what I can say is that we have developed a relationship where we can address our choices and blunders with grace and sensibility and we can resolve them with love, communication, and compassion. We honor and respect one another as well as our promises. And I think most importantly, each of us is able to look at the world, each other, and ourselves to see the Unique Brilliance in it all.

That is my story. Now I would like to invite you to write YOUR ending to this journal. Make up your own "Afterword" and tell the world what you have learned and accomplished as a result of realizing your greatness. I am standing for the Unique Brilliance in You.

My Afterword

TreeNeutral

Advantage Media Group is proud to be a part of the Tree Neutral™ program. Tree Neutral offsets the number of trees consumed in the production and printing of this book by taking proactive steps such as planting trees in direct proportion to the number of trees used to print books. To learn more about Tree Neutral, please visit **www.treeneutral. com.** To learn more about Advantage Media Group's commitment to being a responsible steward of the environment, please visit **www. advantagefamily.com/green**

Stop Raising Einstein is available in bulk quantities at special discounts for corporate, institutional, and educational purposes. To learn more about the special programs Advantage Media Group offers, please visit **www.KaizenUniversity.com** or call 1.866.775.1696.

Advantage Media Group is a leading publisher of business, motivation, and self-help authors. Do you have a manuscript or book idea that you would like to have considered for publication? Please visit **www.amgbook.com**

Printed in the USA
CPSIA information can be obtained
at www.ICGtesting.com
JSHW012040140824
68134JS00033B/3180

9 781599 321738